Gun Laws

By John Ziff

ELDORADO INK

MAR -- 2015

Eldorado Ink
PO Box 100097
Pittsburgh, PA 15233
www.eldoradoink.com

Produced by OTTN Publishing, Stockton, New Jersey

CPSIA compliance information: Batch#RGO2014-1.
For further information, contact Eldorado Ink at info@eldoradoink.com.

First printing

1 3 5 7 9 8 6 4 2

Library of Congress Cataloging-in-Publication Data

Ziff, John, author.
 Gun laws / John Ziff.
      pages cm. — (Responsible gun ownership)
   Includes bibliographical references and index.
      ISBN 978-1-61900-049-0 (hc)
      ISBN 978-1-61900-055-1 (trade)
      ISBN 978-1-61900-061-2 (ebook)
  1. Firearms—Law and legislation—United States—Juvenile literature.
  2. Gun control—United States—Juvenile literature. I. Title.
   KF3941.Z54 2014
   344.7305'33—dc23

                                          2014000392

*For information about custom editions, special sales, or premiums,
please contact our special sales department at info@eldoradoink.com.*

Table of Contents

Chapter 1

A Patchwork of Laws

Gun ownership is ingrained in American culture. Civilians in the United States hold an estimated 270 million firearms. That's almost nine guns for every 10 people—men, women, and children—in the country. No other nation comes close to the United States in the rate of civilian gun ownership or in the total number of firearms in circulation.

But numbers don't tell the full story. For many Americans, a firearm is more than a tool for hunting, target shooting, or personal protection. It's a symbol of self-reliance. Some gun owners even view the right to bear arms—a right enshrined in the U.S. Constitution—as a crucial bulwark against government tyranny. That's the context for the assertion by Senator Orrin Hatch of Utah, former chairman of the Senate Judiciary Committee, that the right to bear arms is the "right most valued by free men."

Gun ownership may be an important and cherished right for Americans, but that right is not absolute. For example, federal law prohibits certain categories of people—such as felons, the mentally ill, and drug addicts—from possessing firearms. It sets rules that regulate

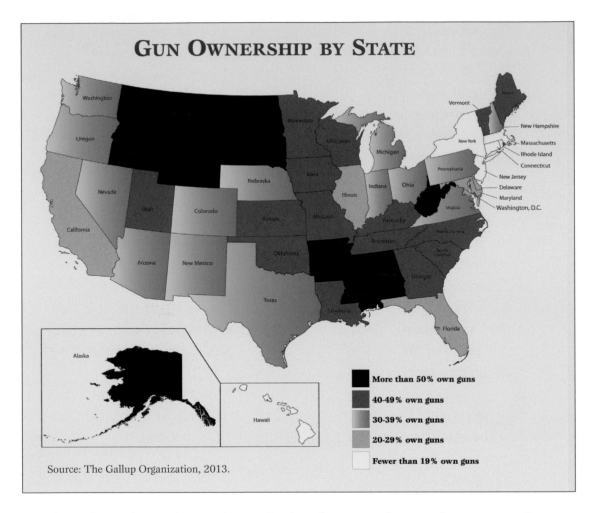

GUN OWNERSHIP BY STATE

- More than 50% own guns
- 40-49% own guns
- 30-39% own guns
- 20-29% own guns
- Fewer than 19% own guns

Source: The Gallup Organization, 2013.

the sale and purchase of certain handguns. It bans other types of firearms altogether.

Although federal gun laws are binding throughout the country, they do not delineate the rights and responsibilities of American gun owners in a comprehensive way. At best, federal laws provide a basic framework for firearms regulation.

To a far greater degree, state laws determine the conditions under which a citizen may legally obtain, carry, and use a firearm. And state gun laws vary widely. A privilege that gun owners in one state take for granted may not be recognized in another. Conduct that is in full compliance with the law may become a violation with the crossing of a state border.

Sometimes, gun laws even vary within a state. Typically, this involves the imposition by large cities of more stringent firearms regulations than exist elsewhere in the state. Many gun rights activists bristle at firearms restrictions generally, but the lack of uniform laws across jurisdictions tends to elicit an especially strong reaction. This situation, gun rights advocates argue, creates confusion and unduly burdens firearms owners. Those who live in, or travel to, jurisdictions with the strictest firearms laws may even be deprived of their fundamental right to defend themselves, gun activists claim.

There is another side to the issue, however. Ensuring public safety is the most basic duty of any government. And when guns are used irresponsibly or criminally, innocent people may—and often do—suffer serious injury or death. So the question becomes, how should the individual's right to have a firearm be balanced with the collective good of minimizing gun violence? Legislators and policy makers in different parts of the country have answered that question differently. The nation's patchwork of gun laws is the result.

A recent case involving two states and one of the country's largest cities highlights many crucial issues in gun policy. It also provides a window into the ever-contentious nature of gun politics.

A PHILADELPHIA STORY

Like other major urban areas, Philadelphia is accustomed to relatively high rates of violent crime. But early 2005 would prove an especially bloody period in the City of Brotherly Love. During a nine-day span in March, Philadelphia suffered a staggering 23 murders.

It was around this time that 23-year-old Marqus Hill received a permit to carry a concealed weapon, or CCW. The permit gave him legal authorization to carry a loaded handgun in public.

Hill lived in the North Philadelphia neighborhood of Hunting Park. Known as a mecca for sellers and buyers of illicit drugs, Hunting Park had one of the highest rates of violent crime in all of Philadelphia. Hardly a day passed without multiple muggings, assaults, or rapes. Nights were often punctuated by gunfire. Though Hunting Park covers just one square mile, it was the scene of six homicides in 2004.

Longtime resident Milta Christian would sum up the feelings of many of her neighbors. "You don't feel safe," she told a TV reporter. "Any place you go you have to be looking around."

For Marqus Hill, however, toting a concealed handgun could bring some peace of mind. As Hill walked the streets of his neighborhood or went to his job with Philadelphia's transit agency, he had a ready means of protecting himself from those who might seek to victimize him.

But on December 21, 2005—a day that saw Philadelphia's homicide toll for the year reach 367—Hill's involvement in a violent altercation led to his arrest. He was charged with attempted murder, aggravated assault, and other offenses. As a result, his concealed-carry permit was revoked.

Hill's case took several years to wend through the legal system. Finally, in 2008, all the criminal charges against him were dropped.

Hill then applied to have his CCW permit reinstated. To his chagrin, he was denied.

"CHARACTER AND REPUTATION"

Pennsylvania's Uniform Firearms Act precludes any city (or other locality) in the commonwealth from enacting its own gun laws. The statute ensures that regardless of where they live or travel in the Keystone State, Pennsylvanians are subject to the same firearms rules. One exception is written into the act: openly carrying a gun in public requires a license only in "cities of the first class," meaning cities with a population of more than one million. Philadelphia is the sole Pennsylvania city in that category.

A permit—the License to Carry Firearms—is necessary everywhere in Pennsylvania in order for a person to legally have a loaded gun in a vehicle or carry one that is concealed while in a public place. Permit applications are processed by the sheriff's office in the applicant's county of residence. The lone exception is Philadelphia, where the police department is responsible for processing applications and maintains a special unit for that purpose.

With regard to concealed-carry permits, Pennsylvania is a "shall issue" state. This means that applicants don't have to demonstrate a particular need to carry a concealed weapon. Rather, an applicant

A state-issued CCW permit allows the gun owner to carry his or her weapon in most areas within that state.

must be issued a permit unless a background check uncovers specific grounds for denial. Those grounds are enumerated in the Pennsylvania Code of Laws. Among the persons the code declares ineligible for a firearms license are: anyone who has been convicted of a felony crime, or who is currently facing a felony charge; drug addicts; people who are habitually drunk; illegal immigrants; anyone who has ever been committed to a mental institution; and any "individual whose character and reputation is such that the individual would be likely to act in a manner dangerous to public safety."

In theory, people seeking a Pennsylvania License to Carry Firearms receive the same consideration regardless of where they apply. In practice, applicants stand a far greater chance of being denied in Philadelphia than elsewhere in Pennsylvania. Statewide, just 1 percent of applications for a firearms permit are rejected. In Philadelphia, the rate is 15 percent.

What explains this huge disparity? In large part, it's a question of differing law enforcement priorities. Philadelphia accounts for about 12 percent of Pennsylvania's total population. Yet in a typical year it records about half of all murders in the state, with the vast majority (more than 80 percent, on average) committed with a gun. And fatal shootings are only part of the story. For every Philadelphian killed by gunfire, five or six others are wounded. In short, Philadelphia suffers

CCW Permit Issuance by State

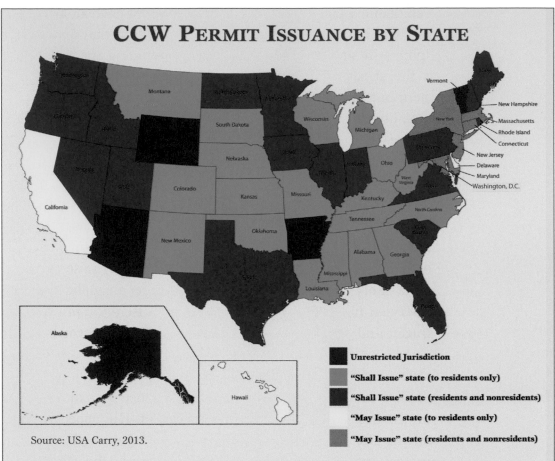

Legend:
- ■ Unrestricted Jurisdiction
- ■ "Shall Issue" state (to residents only)
- ■ "Shall Issue" state (residents and nonresidents)
- □ "May Issue" state (to residents only)
- ■ "May Issue" state (residents and nonresidents)

Source: USA Carry, 2013.

As of 2014, every state allows its citizens to apply for a permit to carry a concealed weapon (CCW). However, the ease or difficulty of actually getting a CCW permit can vary greatly from state to state. In this respect, states can be divided into three categories. *Unrestricted jurisdictions* allow residents to carry a handgun without requiring them to apply for a permit.

Shall-issue states are those in which the responsible agency or authority must issue a CCW permit to anyone who meets the criteria for the permit. The criteria may include a minimum age, proof of residency in the state, passage of a background check, and/or completion of a firearm safety class. Some shall-issue states only grant permits to residents; others grant permits to nonresidents as well.

May-issue states also require CCW permit applicants to fulfill certain criteria. However, in these jurisdictions local or state law enforcement officials have discretion to decide whether or not to issue the permit. These states typically require gun owners to show "good cause" before they will grant a CCW permit.

There are certain parts of the United States where private citizens are not allowed to carry concealed weapons. These *no-issue jurisdiction*s include the District of Columbia, as well as overseas territories such as Puerto Rico, the U.S. Virgin Islands, and American Samoa. In addition, federal laws prohibit private citizens from carrying handguns on school property or bringing them onto military bases or into federal government buildings, including post offices.

from an epidemic of gun violence. No county in Pennsylvania—which is a largely rural state—has a gun violence problem that approaches Philadelphia's in severity. Not surprisingly, reducing the number of guns on the streets is a major concern of the Philadelphia Police Department but generally not for Pennsylvania county sheriffs.

This reality can be seen in the treatment of CCW applications. Everyone seeking a CCW permit in Pennsylvania undergoes a background check that includes searches of five state and three federal databases. But in Philadelphia, all permit applicants must complete an additional questionnaire and sit for a face-to-face interview with a member of the Philadelphia Police Department's standalone Gun Permits Unit. Past contacts with police are investigated, even if the applicant was never charged with a crime. Should this added scrutiny raise concerns about public safety, the Gun Permits Unit may reject an application that would otherwise have been approved, using the discretion provided by the "character and reputation" clause of Pennsylvania firearms law.

MAIL-ORDER PERMIT

Marqus Hill found the reinstatement of his concealed-carry permit denied on the basis of that subjective assessment. Hill appealed. At a 2008 hearing, after the judge upheld the decision to deny his permit, Hill launched into an expletive-laced tirade inside the courtroom. When a police officer attempted to calm him down, Hill punched the officer. This led to an assault charge.

Ultimately, prosecutors offered Hill a plea bargain, and he accepted. He pled guilty to disorderly conduct, a misdemeanor. Though the plea deal had allowed him to avoid a felony record, Hill now stood almost no chance of ever being issued a concealed-carry permit in Philadelphia.

It didn't matter. By 2009 Marqus Hill was again carrying a concealed handgun on the streets of Philadelphia—and doing so legally. Hill had obtained a permit from Florida, and because Pennsylvania had a concealed-carry reciprocity agreement with the Sunshine State, police in Philadelphia were required to honor that permit.

Most states recognize concealed-carry permits issued by at least some other states. Reciprocity arrangements allow people issued a permit in one state to carry their gun legally when they travel to another state. Roughly half of U.S. states issue concealed-carry permits to qualified nonresidents. Requirements vary by state.

Florida has long been known as one of the easiest states from which to obtain a nonresident firearms license. It is among just a handful of states that will issue a license to people who don't apply for or, in some cases, even qualify for a CCW permit in their home state. There is no requirement that an out-of-state applicant work or own a business in Florida. Nor is any in-person appearance necessary; applications can be processed entirely through the mail. Along with the fee of $112, an applicant must submit a completed and notarized application form, a full set of fingerprints, a passport-style photo, and certification that he or she has taken a firearms-instruction class.

Critics charge that the Sunshine State has a spotty record when it comes to vetting nonresident permit applicants. The Florida Department of Law Enforcement (FDLE) performs background checks, but responsibility for firearms licensing rests with a state agency, the Department of Agriculture and Consumer Services. Because it isn't a law enforcement agency, the Department of Agriculture may not receive information from the National Instant Criminal Background Check System (NICS). For this reason, the FDLE doesn't access NICS—which contains important records that are not in other databases—when performing background checks on CCW applicants.

Through a negotiated reciprocal agreement, two states may commit to honoring each other's CCW permits. As of 2014, a total of 37 states had CCW reciprocity with at least one other state. Florida, Oklahoma, Alaska, Michigan, and Missouri had the most reciprocal agreements in place with other states. An interactive map that shows which state's CCW permits are honored in a particular state is available online at http://www.usacarry.com/concealed_carry_permit_reciprocity_maps.html#concealed-carry-reciprocity.

DECISIONS OVERRIDDEN

Officials in Philadelphia had other reasons to object to Florida's non-resident-permitting procedures. In doing background checks, Florida looks at convictions but not arrests. "If somebody has been arrested a dozen times and the cases have just been dismissed or discharged, that doesn't mean the crime didn't happen," noted Lt. Lisa King, commander of the Philadelphia Police Department's Gun Permits Unit.

Nor does Florida make any attempt to ascertain whether out-of-state CCW applicants have been denied a permit, or had their permit revoked, in their home state. "[Someone] could be disapproved here and they could apply in Florida and we are not notified," Lt. King complained. "So if we are not giving them a permit to carry, how is Florida allowed to override our decision?"

Officials in Philadelphia argued that their citizens were put at risk because Florida approved CCW licenses for people who'd been denied by the Gun Permits Unit. People like Shykeem Leslie, a suspected drug dealer with three prior felony arrests, for robbery, aggravated assault, and distribution of illegal drugs. People like Rafiq Williams, identified as the person who raked a North Philadelphia street corner with gunfire one summer night, killing one teen and wounding another. Williams was acquitted after the wounded youth, who'd expressed concern for his family's safety, recanted his testimony on the witness stand. People like Marqus Hill.

On the morning of September 12, 2010, Hill was at his girlfriend's apartment in North Philadelphia when he heard a car alarm. Going outside to investigate, he saw three youths breaking into his car. He didn't call police. Instead, he pulled out his handgun, approached the vehicle, and pumped 13 rounds into Irving Santana, killing the 18-year-old. Hill later pled guilty to third-degree murder and was sentenced to 8 to 20 years in prison.

CLOSING THE "FLORIDA LOOPHOLE"

The Santana slaying was just one of many crimes cited by Philadelphia police and prosecutors in which the perpetrators had Florida nonresident CCW licenses. Calls for the abolishment of the so-called Florida loophole mounted. In February 2013 Pennsylvania's recently elected attorney general, Kathleen Kane, changed the terms of the Keystone State's gun reciprocity agreement with Florida. Kane declared that a Florida-issued CCW license would now be honored in Pennsylvania only if the permit holder maintained residences in both states. Pennsylvanians with Florida permits would have 120 days to obtain a permit in the Keystone State.

Kane's decision, and the deeply divided reaction it provoked, illustrates America's gun debate in microcosm. On one side, advocates of gun control praised the attorney general for taking what they viewed as commonsense action to protect the public.

"Why would we allow officials in another state to decide which Pennsylvanians may carry a concealed weapon in Pennsylvania?" Philadelphia district attorney Seth Williams asked. "General Kane correctly recognizes that it is bad policy to cede important law enforcement decisions to officials who know nothing about Pennsylvania from other states."

Gun rights advocates, by contrast, expressed outrage at the attorney general's decision. They insisted that the new rules wouldn't reduce gun-related crime—criminals would carry concealed weapons regardless—but would merely burden law-abiding citizens. "Why make it harder for us?" complained Philadelphia resident Randy Huggins, a Florida permit holder. "Make it harder for the criminals. Leave us alone."

Joseph Oliver, a Philadelphia-based firearms instructor, shared that sentiment. "You can purchase a firearm," he said, "but you can't get a permit in Philadelphia to save your life. That's what causes people to go to other states to get the permits." Oliver maintained that some of his students had been denied concealed-carry permits on the basis of unpaid child support or traffic tickets, which he considered outrageous. Another skirmish in America's long-running gun wars loomed.

Chapter 2

Federal Gun Laws: A Brief History

rom the earliest days of the Republic, state and local governments regulated the possession and use of firearms. Before the 20th century, however, only a handful of federal gun laws were enacted.

The Second Amendment to the U.S. Constitution, ratified in 1791, reads in full: "A well regulated Militia, being necessary to the security of a free State, the right of the people to keep and bear Arms, shall not be infringed." Today, more than two centuries later, the precise meaning of those 27 words is still disputed.

In 1792 Congress passed, and President George Washington signed, legislation that actually *required* every free, able-bodied white male citizen between the ages of 18 and 45 to own a musket or rifle, and to keep a specified amount of ammunition and gunpowder. The measure was designed to help ensure that the citizen militia would be prepared for military service in the event of a national emergency. At the time, the United States maintained only a small standing army, about 5,000 men in all.

In England, as well as in the American colonies, civilians were expected to own weapons and use them when called to defend the nation. Citizen militias played a role in the Revolutionary War, most famously at the battles of Lexington and Concord (depicted here). The U.S. Constitution preserved the militia tradition, and the Second Amendment ensured that private citizens would have the necessary firearms if they were called up. Constitutional scholars disagree on whether the amendment was intended to confer an individual right to own guns independent of militia service, but the Supreme Court recently decided that it does.

THE FREEDMEN'S BUREAU ACT

The 1792 law didn't apply to blacks, and the clear but unstated reason for this was slavery. Whites in the South lived in constant fear of slave insurrections. They weren't about to mandate that black men, even free black men, own firearms. In fact, state and local statutes throughout most of the South expressly forbade any black to have a gun.

The Civil War finally ended slavery, but it didn't end the determination of many white Southerners to continue oppressing the black population. By the end of 1865, Southern states had begun promulgating the so-called Black Codes. In most places these laws, which restricted the civil rights of newly freed slaves, included a ban on gun ownership by African Americans. Roving bands of white Southerners confiscated the guns their black neighbors had acquired. This left black families virtually helpless to defend themselves against violence, intimidation, and depredation committed by armed whites.

In response to this situation, the U.S. Congress in July 1866 passed the Freedmen's Bureau Act. It mandated that former slaves enjoy the "full and equal benefit of all laws and proceedings concerning personal liberty . . . including the constitutional right to bear arms."

FIRST STEPS TOWARD GUN CONTROL

For different reasons, both the Militia Act of 1792 and the Freedmen's Bureau Act of 1866 sought to expand gun ownership among certain groups of Americans. By contrast, federal gun laws in the 20th century were enacted mainly to limit firearms in the United States. Often these laws came in response to notorious incidents of gun violence.

By the early 1930s, spurred in large part by opportunities created by Prohibition, organized crime had become a highly visible problem. Mob bosses carved out criminal fiefdoms in many of the nation's cities. Turf battles were waged—frequently in public places—with weapons like the Thompson submachine gun. Originally designed for military use, this rapid-fire, fully automatic rifle could be fitted with a 50-round drum magazine.

The fearsome firepower of the "Tommy gun" also made it a favorite of some of the most infamous bank robbers of the era, including John Dillinger, Clyde Barrow and Bonnie Parker, and Baby Face Nelson. Local police often found themselves hopelessly outgunned.

Congress responded to the rampant outlaw violence by passing the nation's first significant gun control legislation, the National Firearms Act of 1934. It targeted "gangster weapons": fully automatic rifles

Notorious bank robbers Bonnie Parker and Clyde Barrow posed for this photo during their 1932–1934 crime spree. Parker is holding a Remington M-11 20-gauge shotgun with a sawed-off barrel and shortened stock. She called the weapon her "whipit," because it could easily be concealed under a long coat and "whipped out" when needed. Such weapons were outlawed by the National Firearms Act of 1934.

such as the Tommy gun, as well as sawed-off shotguns and short-barreled rifles, which were easily concealed under a coat. In the view of lawmakers, such weapons had no legitimate private use.

The law didn't ban the weapons outright. Rather, it imposed a tax of $200—which was then a large sum—each time ownership of a covered weapon was transferred, and it required that the firearm be registered. Violations were punishable by a steep fine and up to five years in prison.

In 1938 Congress passed additional gun control measures in the Federal Firearms Act. It required firearms manufacturers and dealers involved in interstate or foreign commerce to obtain, for a nominal annual fee, a federal license. It also required gun dealers to keep records of their sales. The act prohibited convicted felons, people under criminal indictment, and fugitives from justice from purchasing guns.

Neither the 1934 nor the 1938 law proved at all controversial, even among gun enthusiasts. Karl Frederick, president of the National Rifle Association (NRA)—the premier organization representing hunters and target shooters—called the gun control measures "reasonable, sensible, and fair legislation." There is no evidence the NRA's rank-and-file members disagreed with that assessment. The story would be quite different the next time Congress took up a gun control bill.

BACKLASH

On November 22, 1963, President John F. Kennedy was assassinated in Dallas. The killer, Lee Harvey Oswald, had purchased the World War II–vintage rifle used in the assassination through a mail-order advertisement in *American Rifleman*, the NRA's magazine.

Less than a week after Kennedy's death, a gun control bill was introduced in the House of Representatives. Its scope was quite limited—the bill would merely restrict mail-order sales of long guns (rifles and shotguns). The NRA initially supported the legislation. "We do not think," NRA executive vice president Franklin L. Orth declared in testimony before Congress, "that any sane American, who calls himself an American, can object to placing into this bill the instrument which killed the president of the United States."

(Left) Lee Harvey Oswald poses in his backyard holding the Mannlicher-Carcano rifle that he had purchased through a mail-order dealer for $21.45 during the spring of 1963. (Right) President Kennedy has just moments to live in this photo taken November 22, 1963. Kennedy's assassination raised interest in federal legislation to regulate the sale and possession of firearms.

Many NRA members vehemently disagreed. Thousands quit the organization in protest. Howls and execrations were directed at Orth and other NRA officers, whose resignations were demanded. Orth even received death threats. In the face of the unexpected backlash, the NRA abandoned its support for the bill, officially taking no position on whether mail-order sales of long guns should be restricted.

Other sportsmen's organizations, however, mobilized their members to oppose the bill. It failed to advance.

Despite the intensity of the opposition aroused by a very modest gun control proposal, the administration of President Lyndon Johnson decided to push for more comprehensive firearms restrictions after Johnson's landslide election victory in 1964.

Many U.S. senators and representatives found themselves in politically uncomfortable territory. While a majority of their constituents might support gun control, a vocal, organized, and increasingly well-

THE EVOLUTION OF THE NRA

Today, the National Rifle Association—which bills itself as the "only firewall standing between . . . firearm freedoms and those who would take them away"—is the country's most prominent gun rights advocacy group. The NRA opposes virtually every measure that might in any way limit firearms ownership. It wasn't always that way.

The NRA was founded in 1871 by William Church and George Wingate, two Civil War veterans who'd been dismayed by the awful marksmanship of many of their Union comrades-in-arms. The NRA's original mission was to improve American men's shooting skills as a matter of military readiness. To that end, Wingate and Church enlisted the former Union general Ambrose Burnside to serve as the NRA's first president, and the organization aided shooting clubs and sponsored competitions.

By the 1920s, the NRA had become involved in legislative efforts to standardize state gun laws—but in the direction of increased firearms regulation. The organization supported the federal gun control laws of the 1930s. While the NRA objected to certain provisions of the Gun Control Act of 1968, the organization's executive vice president declared that "the measure as a whole appears to be one that the sportsmen of America can live with."

But sportsmen such as hunters and target shooters represented a declining proportion of the NRA's membership. More and more members owned firearms (especially handguns) for self-protection, and they tended to be staunchly opposed to gun control.

At the annual membership meeting in 1977, a group of hardline gun rights advocates engineered a takeover of the NRA's board of directors. Since then the NRA has lobbied for gun laws consistent with the broadest possible interpretation of the Second Amendment.

As of mid-2013, the NRA claimed about 5 million members.

funded interest group—what would come to be called the "gun lobby"—opposed it. Most members of Congress found it prudent to avoid taking a definitive stance either way. For several years, gun control legislation remained stalled in congressional committees. A series of shocking events would eventually change the political calculus.

The Gun Control Act of 1968

In July 1967 deadly race riots tore through Detroit and Newark, New Jersey. In both cases, police and National Guard troops came under fire when they tried to put down the disturbances. In one neighborhood on Detroit's east side, armed rioters held the authorities at bay for three full days.

A federal report issued in 1968 found that the high number of guns in circulation had helped ignite and sustain the riots—and would put other American cities at risk for large-scale civil unrest. The report's authors drew "the firm conclusion that effective firearms controls are an essential contribution to domestic peace and tranquility."

On April 4, 1968, a white supremacist used a hunting rifle to kill civil rights leader Martin Luther King Jr. in Memphis, Tennessee. The assassination touched off riots in more than 100 cities. As had been the case in Detroit and Newark the previous year,

These New York police officers have drawn their guns during a 1960s race riot in Harlem. The 1960s were a time of social turmoil in the United States. An increase in the level of gun-related violence led American policy makers to call for new restrictions on gun ownership.

Armed members of the National Guard patrol the streets of Washington, D.C., after rioting that followed the assassination of civil rights leader Martin Luther King Jr. in April 1968. The murders of King and presidential candidate Robert Kennedy created a climate of support for gun control legislation, including restrictions on certain types of handguns.

rioters in many of these cities fired on police and National Guardsmen.

Momentum was building for gun control legislation. One more national trauma would push the legislation across the finish line. Shortly after midnight on June 6, 1968, a handgun-wielding assassin killed Senator Robert F. Kennedy, a Democratic candidate for president, at a Los Angeles hotel. In Washington later that same day, Congress passed the Omnibus Crime Control and Safe Streets Act (OCCSSA), which contained the first new gun control measures since the Federal Firearms Act of 1938.

A few months later, on October 22, President Johnson signed the Gun Control Act of 1968. Together with the OCCSSA, the Gun Control Act (GCA) overhauled the nation's firearms laws. It prohibited interstate sales of all firearms. It banned the importation of surplus military weapons. It also banned the importation of certain cheap and popular handguns, known colloquially as "Saturday night specials," that were deemed to be unsuitable for any sporting purpose. The GCA expanded the categories of people ineligible to possess any firearm to include illegal-drug users and any person who'd ever been adjudicated "mentally defective" or committed to a mental institution.

The GCA required all gun dealers to obtain a federal firearms

"Saturday night special" refers broadly to any small, inexpensive handgun. The term was first coined by police in Detroit, who observed that an increase in weekend shootings was closely associated with the availability of these weapons.

license, even if they sold only weapons manufactured in their own state. Previously, no license had been needed in the absence of interstate commerce. The new law defined a gun dealer as anyone who on a full- or part-time basis devoted "time, attention, and labor to dealing in firearms as a regular course of trade or business with the principal objective of livelihood or profit."

Under the GCA, eligibility requirements for a federal license to sell firearms weren't difficult to meet: the applicant merely had to be at least 21 years old, have nonresidential premises from which to conduct business, and not personally be disqualified from possessing guns. However, federal firearms licensees (FFLs) were obliged to verify the eligibility of all prospective purchasers. That meant checking photo ID to confirm that the buyer was an in-state resident and met age requirements (21 for the purchase of a handgun, 18 for a long gun). In addition, the FFL had to collect a signed statement in which the purchaser attested that he or she was eligible to own a firearm.

Gun control advocates predicted that the GCA would lead to a significant reduction in firearms-related crime. Most criminologists, however, believe the law's actual effects were modest at best.

Several key omissions in the GCA undermined its intended goals. For example, an FFL had no obligation to check the veracity of a prospective buyer's statement that he or she was eligible to own a gun. The ban on imported Saturday night specials didn't prevent domestic gun manufacturers from churning out those weapons. The ban on imported military surplus rifles could be circumvented by importing parts and assembling the weapons in the United States. Perhaps most critically, the gun lobby had succeeded in getting stripped from the final version of the GCA provisions that would have required firearms buyers to register their weapons and to be licensed.

THE FIREARMS OWNERS' PROTECTION ACT

During the 1970s, gun rights advocates grew increasingly dissatisfied with the implementation of the GCA. They asserted that the agency charged with administering federal gun laws—the Bureau of Alcohol, Tobacco, and Firearms (ATF)—trampled the rights of law-abiding gun owners with overzealous enforcement policies and burdened FFLs with onerous recordkeeping requirements. A campaign was begun to roll back the GCA, with the National Rifle Association taking the lead role.

The gun rights camp claimed a partial victory in 1986, when Congress passed and President Ronald Reagan signed the Firearms Owners' Protection Act (FOPA). The law was a boon for firearms dealers. Failure to keep the required records for gun sales was changed from a felony offense to a misdemeanor, and the ATF couldn't conduct more than one unannounced inspection of an FFL per year. FOPA allowed FFLs to sell their wares not just at their permanent place of business, but also at temporary events in the same state. This led to explosive growth in the popularity of gun shows. FOPA expressly prohibited the federal government from creating a registry of guns, gun owners, or gun transactions.

At the same time, FOPA did contain a few gun control provisions. It outlawed any future manufacturing of machine guns by private individuals, and it effectively prohibited transfers of existing automatic weapons after 1986. FOPA also made it a crime to knowingly provide a firearm to any individual legally forbidden to own one.

THE BRADY ACT

Arguably the most consequential federal gun control statute ever enacted, the Brady Handgun Violence Prevention Act had its genesis in an assassination attempt. On March 30, 1981, as President Reagan emerged from a hotel in Washington, D.C., where he'd just given a speech, a gunman opened fire from the assembled crowd. Four people

Secret Service agents surround President Reagan (left) after he was shot outside the Washington Hilton Hotel. Reagan's press secretary, James Brady (in blue business suit), and policeman Thomas Delahanty lie wounded on the sidewalk.

were wounded: Reagan, a Secret Service agent, a D.C. police officer, and James Brady, the president's press secretary. Brady, shot in the head, was not expected to survive.

Investigators soon discovered that the would-be assassin, 25-year-old John Hinckley Jr., had a history of psychiatric problems and was taking antidepressant medications. The previous October, Hinckley had been arrested at an airport in Nashville, Tennessee, for illegal possession of firearms; he'd tried to board a flight with three handguns and 30 rounds of ammunition in his carry-on luggage. Several days after that incident, Hinckley purchased the .22-caliber revolver he would use in the Reagan assassination attempt at a Dallas pawnshop. He listed a false home address on the required paperwork. But the proprietor of the pawnshop was only legally obligated to verify that

Former White House press secretary James Brady (left) watches President Bill Clinton sign into law the Handgun Violence Prevention Act on November 30, 1993.

Hinckley was a state resident, and Hinckley produced an old Texas driver's license.

Gun control advocates said the case exposed a glaring gap in U.S. firearms regulation: the system relied on prospective gun buyers to be truthful. Lying on a firearms application was a felony. But clearly the possibility of future punishment wouldn't deter everybody who was ineligible to own a gun yet eager to acquire one.

Sarah Brady, the wife of President Reagan's former press secretary, championed the push to tighten the rules for gun purchases. Her husband, partially paralyzed from his head wound, became a powerful symbol for this cause. In 1987, six years after John Hinckley's assassination attempt, legislation dubbed the Brady Bill was first introduced in Congress. It called for a mandatory background check, to be performed by law enforcement, for everyone who sought to buy a handgun from an FFL (except purchasers who had a valid firearms permit). Conducting such background checks would take time, necessitating a waiting period between a prospective buyer's application and his or her actual receipt of the weapon. The Brady Bill specified a waiting period of seven days.

That provision especially rankled gun rights advocates, and opposition to the bill proved fierce. The NRA alone spent millions of dollars lobbying against the legislation. The bill died, only to be reintroduced, in three successive Congresses. Supporters finally gained the upper hand in 1993.

The Brady Handgun Violence Prevention Act, signed into law by President Bill Clinton on November 30, 1993, followed the basic outlines of the original Brady Bill. It did, however, incorporate several

OTHER NOTABLE FEDERAL FIREARMS LAWS

Armed Career Criminal Act of 1984—Established a mandatory minimum prison sentence of 15 years for possession of a firearm by anyone with three prior felony convictions for robbery or burglary (or, as amended in 1986, three prior convictions for any violent felonies or serious drug charges).

Law Enforcement Officers Protection Act of 1986—Banned the manufacture, importation, and sale of armor-piercing bullets (widely known as "cop killer" ammunition).

Undetectable Firearms Act of 1988—Banned any firearm not detectable with a metal detector or X-ray machine, such as one made of plastic.

Assault Weapons Ban (1994)—Part of the Violent Crime and Law Enforcement Act, it prohibited the manufacture of 18 specific semiautomatic firearms, in addition to any firearm with certain military-style features (such as a bayonet mount or flash suppressor). Any firearms manufactured before the law went into effect remained legal to own or sell, however. The assault weapons ban expired in 2004.

compromises designed to win support from gun rights proponents. The waiting period was reduced to five days. More important, the law mandated the eventual elimination of waiting periods; it required that a system for instant background checks be in place within five years. In the interim, only handgun purchases would be subject to background checks. After the permanent provisions of the law took effect, on November 30, 1998, all firearms purchases from FFLs would be covered.

Legal challenges to the Brady Act, bankrolled largely by the NRA, arose almost immediately. Until the federally administered National Instant Criminal Background Check System (NICS) was set up, the act required local chief law enforcement officers to conduct background checks. County sheriffs in Montana and Arizona objected, claiming that Congress lacked the authority to compel them to perform federal duties, even on a temporary basis. The issue ultimately landed before the U.S. Supreme Court. In 1997, in the case of *Printz v. United States*, the Court ruled unconstitutional the Brady Act's requirement that local law enforcement officers perform background checks. But the justices declined to invalidate the entire law, as the NRA had urged.

The Supreme Court's decision had little practical effect. In most states, officials continued to perform background checks voluntarily. And NICS went online the following year.

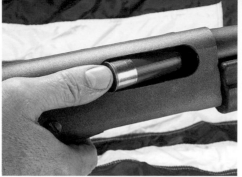

Chapter 3

Keeping Guns Out of the Wrong Hands

In most parts of the United States, buying a gun is simple and convenient. Go to a gun shop, a sporting goods store, a Walmart, or another establishment with a federal license to sell firearms. Pick out the gun or guns you wish to buy. Present a valid driver's license or other government-issued photo ID. Fill out the first page of Form 4473, providing basic information (name, address, date and place of birth, and so on) and answering a dozen yes-or-no questions. Sign the document. Wait while your instant background check is performed. If you're approved, pay for your weapons and be on your way.

The entire process could take as little as 10 or 15 minutes. And NICS is what makes that sort of convenience possible.

HOW NICS WORKS

Under the Brady Act, FFLs are responsible for initiating background checks. In most states this means directly contacting NICS, which is run by the Federal Bureau of Investigation, either by phone or via the Internet. However, some states have

U.S. Department of Justice
Bureau of Alcohol, Tobacco, Firearms and Explosives

OMB No. 1140-0020

Firearms Transaction Record Part I - Over-the-Counter

WARNING: You may not receive a firearm if prohibited by Federal or State law. The information you provide will be used to determine whether you are prohibited under law from receiving a firearm. Certain violations of the Gun Control Act, 18 U.S.C. §§ 921 et. seq., are punishable by up to 10 years imprisonment and/or up to a $250,000 fine.	Transferor's Transaction Serial Number (If any)

Prepare in original only. All entries must be handwritten in ink. Read the Notices, Instructions, and Definitions on this form. "PLEASE PRINT."

Section A - Must Be Completed Personally By Transferee (Buyer)

1. Transferee's Full Name
Last Name / First Name / Middle Name (If no middle name, state "NMN")

2. Current Residence Address (U.S. Postal abbreviations are acceptable. Cannot be a post office box.)
Number and Street Address / City / County / State / ZIP Code

3. Place of Birth U.S. City and State -OR- Foreign Country	4. Height Ft. ___ In. ___	5. Weight (Lbs.)	6. Gender ☐ Male ☐ Female	7. Birth Date Month Day Year

8. Social Security Number (Optional, but will help prevent misidentification)   9. Unique Personal Identification Number (UPIN) if applicable (See Instructions for Question 9.)

10.a. Ethnicity
☐ Hispanic or Latino
☐ Not Hispanic or Latino

10.b. Race (Check one or more boxes.)
☐ American Indian or Alaska Native   ☐ Black or African American   ☐ White
☐ Asian   ☐ Native Hawaiian or Other Pacific Islander

11. Answer questions 11.a. (see exceptions) through 11.l. and 12 (if applicable) by checking or marking "yes" or "no" in the boxes to the right of the questions.

	Yes	No
a. Are you the actual transferee/buyer of the firearm(s) listed on this form? Warning: You are not the actual buyer if you are acquiring the firearm(s) on behalf of another person. If you are not the actual buyer, the dealer cannot transfer the firearm(s) to you. (See Instructions for Question 11.a.) Exception: If you are picking up a repaired firearm(s) for another person, you are not required to answer 11.a. and may proceed to question 11.b.	☐	☐
b. Are you under indictment or information in any court for a felony, or any other crime, for which the judge could imprison you for more than one year? (See Instructions for Question 11.b.)	☐	☐
c. Have you ever been convicted in any court of a felony, or any other crime, for which the judge could have imprisoned you for more than one year, even if you received a shorter sentence including probation? (See Instructions for Question 11.c.)	☐	☐
d. Are you a fugitive from justice?	☐	☐
e. Are you an unlawful user of, or addicted to, marijuana or any depressant, stimulant, narcotic drug, or any other controlled substance?	☐	☐
f. Have you ever been adjudicated mentally defective (which includes a determination by a court, board, commission, or other lawful authority that you are a danger to yourself or to others or are incompetent to manage your own affairs) OR have you ever been committed to a mental institution? (See Instructions for Question 11.f.)	☐	☐
g. Have you been discharged from the Armed Forces under dishonorable conditions?	☐	☐
h. Are you subject to a court order restraining you from harassing, stalking, or threatening your child or an intimate partner or child of such partner? (See Instructions for Question 11.h.)	☐	☐

A firearms transaction record, or Form 4473, must be filled out when you purchase any firearm from a federally licensed dealer.

agreed to serve as a liaison, or point of contact (POC) for NICS, and in those states the FFL contacts a designated state agency to initiate a background check.

In non-POC states, the FFL phones an FBI call center, where an employee codes in the information from the prospective buyer's Form 4473, or the FFL uploads the completed form using NICS E-Check. A computerized search of three national databases ensues. Those databases are the Interstate Identification Index, which maintains criminal history records; the National Crime Information Center, which includes files on individuals who are the subject of a protection order or an active criminal warrant; and the NICS Index, which contains information contributed by local, state, and federal agencies about individuals ineligible to possess a firearm. If the prospective buyer isn't a U.S. citizen, U.S. Immigration and Customs Enforcement databases are also searched.

In all, a computerized NICS check searches more than 75 million records, which usually takes about 30 seconds. If no records are found matching the prospective buyer, the FFL is immediately notified that the sale may proceed. This happens about 70 percent of the time. If, however, the system does return a possible match, the FFL is notified that the sale is delayed. The phone call or electronic form is transferred to the NICS Section, located within the headquarters of the FBI's Criminal Justice Information Services Division in Clarksburg,

West Virginia. There a NICS examiner reviews the information to determine whether the possible match is valid. Often it isn't—the prospective buyer may, for example, simply have the same name as someone with a criminal record. Usually the examiner can make a definitive determination within minutes, and the FFL is notified that the sale may proceed or is denied. Approximately 92 percent of instant background checks are resolved by this stage.

For the remaining 8 percent or so, further investigation is required, and the FFL is instructed to delay the sale. Under the Brady Act, the NICS Section has three business days to contact the FFL with a decision. Otherwise, the sale may legally proceed pending a final determination, which must come within 88 days. If, during that period, the NICS Section finds that the buyer should have been denied a firearm, it notifies the Bureau of Alcohol, Tobacco, and Firearms. ATF agents then attempt to retrieve the weapon. Whenever a background check results in a denial, the person may appeal the decision.

FFLs are required to keep permanent records of gun sales, but the Brady Act limits the government's recordkeeping. Firearms applica-

The NICS Section is located at the FBI's Criminal Justice Information Services Division in Clarksburg, West Virginia. To initiate a background check, FFLs contact the NICS Section via a toll-free telephone number or electronically through NICS E-Check. The descriptive information provided on the ATF Form 4473 is used in a search of multiple databases.

NICS BY THE NUMBERS

Background checks conducted: 174,623,643

Applications denied (Nov. 30, 1998–2010):

    By state and local agencies: 2.1%

    By the FBI's NICS Section: 1.4%

Total denials by NICS Section: 1,044,050

Reason for NICS Section denials:

    Felony conviction/misdemeanor conviction punishable by more than two years: 57.65%

    Misdemeanor conviction, domestic violence: 10.05%

    Fugitive from justice: 10.04%

    Unlawful user/addicted to controlled substance: 8.32%

    Prohibited by state law: 4.60%

    Domestic violence protection/restraining order: 4.23%

    Under indictment/information: 2.15%

    Other: 2.96%

Denials reversed on appeal (2000–2010):

    FBI: 33,586

    State: 72,941 (Some states didn't report for all years.)

Note: Unless otherwise indicated, figures are for Nov. 30, 1998, to Aug. 31, 2013.
Sources: FBI, Bureau of Justice Statistics.

tions must be deleted from the NICS system within 24 hours of approval (or at the end of the 88-day extended-investigation period, regardless of whether a definitive determination on the applicant's eligibility has been made). The FBI retains only records of firearms applications that are denied. The Brady Act expressly prohibits any government agency from setting up a registry of firearms or firearms owners.

According to the FBI, nearly 175 million firearms background checks (including those associated with permit requests) were conducted through NICS between November 30, 1998, and August 31, 2013. State POC users accounted for about 53 percent of these checks; the NICS Section, about 47 percent. In all, more than 2.1 million firearms applications were denied. The most common disqualifying factor was conviction of a felony crime.

FALSE POSITIVES

How effective is the instant background check in keeping guns "out of the wrong hands"? The system has skeptics from both sides of the gun divide.

Many gun rights advocates insist that NICS does little to prevent criminals from obtaining firearms but merely places a burden on law-abiding citizens. These critics decry what they regard as an unacceptably high number of "false positives"—people who are erroneously identified as ineligible to own a firearm. John Lott, an economist and supporter of the controversial idea that increased firearms ownership reduces crime, has attempted to calculate the rate of false positives produced by NICS. Using data from 2009, Lott puts the rate in excess of 94 percent. He arrives at this startling figure indirectly. Intentionally providing false information on a firearms application is a felony. Yet less than 2 percent of the people denied a firearm in 2009 were prosecuted. Even assuming that prosecutors declined to pursue some cases because, for example, they believed the applicant had made an honest mistake on Form 4473, Lott concludes that the low rate of prosecutions means that the overwhelming majority of NICS denials were erroneous. "How hard is it," he asks, "for prosecutors to prove

Under section 922(g) of the Brady Handgun Violence Prevention Act, a person who has been convicted of a felony is prohibited from owning firearms. Crimes classified as felonies include murder, rape, aggravated assault, arson, burglary, fraud, grand theft, drug dealing, perjury, and other serious offenses.

that someone hadn't accidentally forgotten a conviction for a violent felony or omitted a restraining order?"

U.S. attorneys, who are responsible for prosecuting NICS violations, contend that it is, in fact, hard to prove that someone hasn't accidentally forgotten information. And in any event, juries are often loath to convict defendants prohibited from owning a firearm when the reason is something other than a violent-felony record. Moreover, prosecutorial resources are limited, and NICS cases typically receive low priority. According to a 2004 report by the Justice Department's inspector general, these factors—rather than an astronomical rate of erroneous firearms denials—explain the minuscule number of NICS prosecutions.

Still, the problem of false positives under NICS does exist. Data from the Bureau of Justice Statistics indicate that between 2000 and 2010, nearly one in five applicants who were denied a firearm appealed the decision. Of this group, 37.6 percent won their appeal. Extrapolating from the total number of background checks run during this period (about 114 million), this means that approximately one of every thousand NICS checks generated a false positive. Obviously, not everyone denied a firearm appealed, so the actual proportion of false positives would certainly be somewhat higher.

GETTING AROUND A BACKGROUND CHECK

If gun rights supporters consider the instant background check onerous and often unfair to people who should be allowed to own a firearm, gun control advocates believe the system is too easily circumvented by people who shouldn't. One important concern is the laxity of some states in entering relevant records, such as mental-institution commitments, into the NICS Index database. A more fundamental issue is the scope of the Brady Act's background check requirements. The law covers only gun sales by federal firearms licensees. A prospective gun buyer who wishes to avoid a background check need only seek out a private seller at a gun show or flea market or on the Internet.

How many legal firearms transactions occur without a background check? As with so many aspects of America's gun debate, the opposing sides disagree even on the basic data. Gun control groups such as Mayors Against Illegal Guns commonly assert that 40 percent of all firearms sales involve unlicensed private sellers and hence take place with no background check. But that figure represents an old estimate based on even older data. The estimate appeared in a 1997 National Institute of Justice (NIJ) study, and it relied on a small sampling of respondents to a survey conducted in 1993 and 1994.

All federally licensed firearms dealers are required to conduct background checks of their customers. However, private individuals are allowed to sell firearms without a background check, so long as this is not the way they make their regular living. In 32 states, there are no restrictions on the sale of firearms at gun shows by private individuals, leading gun control advocates to complain that this is an easy and legal way for criminals to procure firearms.

Asked in 2012 whether the 40 percent estimate was still valid, Philip Cook, one of the coauthors of the NIJ study, replied, "The answer is I have no idea."

"It is hard to believe that it is above single digits," John Lott says of the percentage of firearms purchased without a background check. For its part, the NRA avoids directly addressing the question, preferring instead to focus on the low proportion of criminals who get weapons from gun shows, flea markets, or other legal venues. The NRA, too, makes use of old data—a 1991 ATF report indicating that 6 percent of "career criminals" obtained firearms from gun shows or flea markets; a 2001 Bureau of Justice Statistics survey of state prison inmates convicted of firearms crimes, which found that just 1.7 percent had gotten their weapon from a flea market or gun show.

Even if it's true that more than 90 percent of firearms sales take place with a background check, or that criminals rarely get firearms from gun shows, proponents of gun control don't regard that as a reason to maintain what they call the "gun-show loophole." Why, they ask, should the law make it easier for *anybody* to get a gun if they're prohibited from owning one? Some state legislatures have accepted the logic of this argument. As of 2013, a total of 10 states, plus the District of Columbia, required background checks for all firearms purchases at gun shows. Another six states required background checks for gun-show sales of handguns only.

Chapter 4

Waiting for the Gun

ederal law doesn't mandate a waiting period for firearms purchases, and NICS makes it possible for most buyers to take immediate possession of a weapon—unless the sale occurs in a state that imposes a waiting period. As of mid-2013, four states and the District of Columbia had a waiting period for all firearms, five states had a waiting period for handguns only, and one state had a waiting period for handguns and assault weapons. State waiting periods range from 24 hours (Illinois, for long guns) to 14 days (Hawaii). The average is about five days.

The primary rationale for a waiting period is that it gives people who might otherwise commit a violent act impulsively the chance to "cool off." Gun rights advocates, however, argue that waiting periods can put law-abiding citizens at risk. Suppose, for example, that a man threatens to kill his estranged wife. She tries to get a handgun to protect herself but must wait for a couple days under the laws of her state. In the meantime, the abusive husband breaks into the woman's home and murders her. This, some gun-rights advocates say, is exactly what happened to a Wisconsin woman named Bonnie Elmasri.

KILLED BY GUN CONTROL?

Elmasri, 38, was in the midst of a divorce and had obtained a court order prohibiting her husband, Mohsen M. Elmasri, from having any contact with her. But according to police, she sometimes allowed him inside her home in Wauwatosa anyway. In March 1991, Mohsen Elmasri entered the home and shot to death his estranged wife and their two children, ages 17 and 3, before killing himself.

"Bonnie had inquired about getting a gun to protect herself from a husband who had repeatedly threatened to kill her," Erich Pratt, communications director for Gun Owners of America (GOA), explained 10 years after the murders. "She was told there was a 48 hour waiting period to buy a handgun. But unfortunately, Bonnie was never able to pick up her gun. She and her two sons were killed the next day by an abusive husband of whom the police were well aware."

The tragic story was soon circulated by the NRA, and several members of Congress cited it in arguing against passage of the Brady Bill in 1991. Gun rights activists continue to point to Bonnie Elmasri's murder as an object lesson on the dangers of gun control.

A MURKY CASE

It's not clear that the Elmasri case had anything to do with gun control, however. In the supercharged atmosphere of American gun politics, the actual details of the case were glossed over, whether inadvertently or intentionally.

The victim-killed-because-of-a-waiting-period narrative began shortly after the murders, when James Fendry, the director of an organization called the Wisconsin Pro-Gun Movement, came forward. Fendry, who also taught firearms courses in the Milwaukee area, said he'd received a phone call from a distraught woman a day or two before the killings. The caller said she needed a gun because her life was in danger. Fendry told her that under Wisconsin law, she would have to wait two days before receiving any handgun she bought. Fendry said the caller was from Wauwatosa, and her first name was Bonnie—which Fendry said he remembered because his wife had a friend named Bonnie from that city. But he couldn't recall the woman's last name.

In the hands of the gun lobby, those sketchy details became the basis of a compelling and unambiguous account of the awful toll exacted by misguided firearms laws. That account included a few dramatic embellishments—for example, that the victim had definitely been killed the day after calling James Fendry, not a day or two after, as the firearms instructor had said. But most of all, the story rested on a big assumption: that the caller named Bonnie, from Wauwatosa (1991 population: approximately 50,000), was in fact Bonnie Elmasri.

Her family said it wasn't. "I believe [Fendry] is either making it up entirely or that somebody called him by the name of Bonnie," Elmasri's brother, Gary Greenberg, told the *Milwaukee Journal*, "but that it was not my sister. My sister would never buy a weapon, never. . . . She did not go to a gun shop. I was very close to her and so were my parents, and we can account for almost every minute of [her final] 48 hours."

Wauwatosa police found no indication that Elmasri had ever sought a gun.

A DEARTH OF EVIDENCE

Given the flimsiness of the evidence—some would say the absence of evidence—it seems peculiar that gun activists would choose the Elmasri case to illustrate the dangers of firearms waiting periods. But they apparently were unable to find another case with the same scenario—and, more than 20 years later, apparently still haven't found one. Obviously this doesn't mean a person seeking a gun for self-protection couldn't be murdered during a waiting period. Nor does it mean that has never happened. It does suggest, however, that at most such cases are exceedingly rare.

On the other hand, it's not clear that waiting periods actually do what their proponents claim. A systematic review, conducted in 2005 by the Task Force on Community Preventive Services, an independent group of public health and prevention experts, found that "the evidence is insufficient to determine the effectiveness of waiting periods for the prevention of suicide, homicide, aggravated assault," and other firearms-related incidents. The group cited the small number, problematic designs, and inconsistent outcomes of available studies.

The paucity of solid scientific research on waiting periods, and on other firearms-related issues, can be explained in large part by gun politics. In the 1980s and 1990s, the federal Centers for Disease Control and Prevention (CDC) funded studies on firearms injuries and deaths. Some of these studies reached conclusions the gun lobby didn't like—for instance, that the presence of a gun in the home significantly increases the chances of homicide by a family member or intimate partner. The NRA condemned such findings as politically motivated, then tapped its allies in Congress to make sure further research into firearms violence would be squelched. In 1996 the U.S. House of Representatives voted to reduce the CDC's budget by the precise amount the CDC had spent on firearms research the previous year. The Senate later restored the money, but only with the proviso that "none of the funds made available for injury prevention and control at the Centers for Disease Control and Prevention may be used to advocate or promote gun control." Federally sponsored gun research sputtered to a virtual halt, as agency heads understood the congressional action as a veiled threat.

Eventually, however, the National Institutes of Health (NIH) quietly began funding studies on the public health consequences of firearms. One study published in 2009 found that subjects carrying a firearm were nearly four and a half times more likely to be shot in an assault than subjects who weren't carrying a gun.

"You'd think that after the CDC had their money revoked, we wouldn't be dealing with this," said Erich Pratt, of the Gun Owners of America.

Congress soon responded with a de facto ban on gun violence research by any agency within the Department of Health and Human Services, including the NIH. In January 2013 President Barack Obama announced that he would order federal agencies to resume scientific research into the causes and prevention of firearms-related violence. Whether such research will have any effect on the nation's gun laws remains an open question.

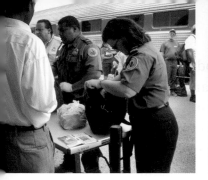

Chapter 5

Ongoing Battles

A fter a brief trip to New York City, Mark Meckler was planning to return to his native California on December 15, 2011. But Meckler, an attorney and cofounder of the conservative political organization Tea Party Patriots, missed his flight. At the Delta Airlines counter in LaGuardia Airport, he tried to check a lockbox containing his Glock pistol and 19 rounds of ammunition. He was promptly arrested and charged with second-degree criminal possession of a weapon—a class C felony carrying a maximum sentence of 15 years in prison.

UNSUSPECTING TRAVELERS

Each year, dozens of visitors to New York City land in the same legal trouble. They have a valid permit to carry a concealed weapon in their home state. They follow their airline's instructions for transporting the handgun—it must be unloaded, inside an approved lockbox, and with checked luggage—and have no difficulty when they arrive in New York City. Only when the visitors attempt to check their weapon for the return flight do they discover they've broken the law.

The state of New York has strict gun control laws, including a requirement that individuals obtain a permit to purchase a handgun, register the weapon, and have a handgun license, even if the weapon is kept in the home. In New York City, whose gun laws are even more restrictive, those requirements apply to long guns as well. It's also very difficult and expensive to obtain a CCW license in New York City.

Under New York's firearms statutes—which are among the most restrictive in the country—it is generally illegal to possess, carry, or transport a handgun anywhere in the state without a New York–issued license. New York doesn't recognize gun permits from any other state. New York City doesn't even recognize permits issued elsewhere in New York State: with a few narrow exceptions, anyone who wants to have a handgun in the Big Apple must get a special permit issued by the New York City Police Department.

New York City prosecutors have shown little inclination to excuse gun-carrying tourists, even when it's clear the visitors weren't deliberately trying to circumvent the rules. "New York gun laws are not exactly a secret," noted Jack Ryan, chief assistant district attorney of Queens. In most cases, however, defendants who were simply unaware of New York's strict gun laws are offered a plea bargain that allows them to avoid a possible felony conviction.

In January 2012, Mark Meckler pled guilty to a misdemeanor count of disorderly conduct and paid a $250 fine. "No one should ever have to go through what my family has been through," he fumed after his hearing, "simply for exercising a fundamental right, specifically enumerated in the United States Constitution."

Meckler's statement notwithstanding, the courts have yet to delineate precisely the extent of the Second Amendment right to bear arms. Supreme Court decisions in *District of Columbia v. Heller* (2008) and *McDonald v. Chicago* (2010) forbid the federal government and state governments, respectively, from completely banning firearms (in particular handguns) kept in the home for self-defense. Less clear, however, is how far governments may go to limit the carrying of firearms in public. That issue will certainly be a focus of court challenges and legislative battles in the coming years.

CARRYING IN PLAIN SIGHT

The vast majority of states allow persons not otherwise prohibited from owning a firearm to openly carry a loaded gun in public places, at least under some conditions. As of July 2013, only three states—California, Florida, and Illinois—along with the District of Columbia completely barred the open carrying of any firearm in public. In three other states (New York, South Carolina, and Texas) it's illegal to tote a handgun around in plain sight, but not a long gun; in three others (Massachusetts, Minnesota, and New Jersey) open carry of handguns is allowed, but open carry of long guns is not. Several other states, including Arkansas, Hawaii, Maryland, and Rhode Island, as well as New Jersey, impose *de facto* bans on open carry.

Of the states that allow the open carrying of handguns, about a

This patron in a Colorado restaurant is openly carrying a 9mm handgun. Colorado law permits "open carry," although the city and county of Denver have passed legislation outlawing this practice in their jurisdictions.

OPEN CARRY LAWS BY STATE

Open Carry prohibited

Open Carry legal with permit

Open Carry permitted

Note: Open Carry may be restricted in certain jurisdictions within a state that otherwise permits the practice.

Source: OpenCarry.org, 2013.

dozen require no permit and have preemption laws, which prohibit local governments from passing ordinances limiting open carry or any other state-recognized gun privileges. An additional dozen states require a license or permit for open carry but also have preemption laws. In the remaining states, open carry is generally legal but may be restricted in certain cities or municipalities.

Every state that allows open carry has restrictions on where gun owners may take their weapons. Schools, government buildings, and bars are almost always off-limits.

A burgeoning open-carry movement has arisen recently among a segment of the gun rights community. Its advocates say they are exercising their Second Amendment rights as America's Founding Fathers intended. They insist that a firearm displayed in plain sight deters crime and signals that the gun owner is law abiding, as criminals typi-cally go to great lengths to hide their weapons.

Opponents, however, maintain that open carry increases the chances for public mayhem. They say that innocent bystanders may be put at risk by inexperienced or careless gun owners, particularly in states where no license or firearms training is required for open carry. Furthermore, when police respond to the inevitable "subject with a gun" calls that open carry generates, how are they to discern the intentions of the person with the firearm? At best, critics argue, law enforcement resources will be wasted; at worst, a deadly confronta-tion might ensue. Even people who are otherwise quite supportive of gun rights have doubts about open carry. The sight of an armed civil-ian walking around a mall, or a fast-food restaurant, or a bowling alley understandably alarms many people. Some gun rights proponents worry that a backlash against open carry might lead to greater support for gun control measures generally.

CONCEALED CARRY

Concealed carry affords the self-defense advantages of having a gun in public, yet isn't provocative in the way openly displaying a firearm tends to be. All 50 states have enacted some form of concealed-carry law. In the District of Columbia, however, carrying a concealed weapon remains illegal.

Illinois, the last state to pass a concealed-carry law, did so in July 2013, under a deadline imposed by the U.S. Seventh Circuit Court of Appeals. That federal court had ruled Illinois' ban on concealed carry unconstitutional, citing the Supreme Court's *Heller* and *McDonald* decisions. While *Heller* and *McDonald* had dealt specifically with firearms in the home, the Seventh Circuit Court believed the implica-tions for the public space were inescapable. "The Supreme Court has decided that the [Second] amendment confers a right to bear arms for self-defense," the judges noted, "which is as important outside the home as inside."

The Seventh Circuit Court handed down its decision in December 2012. Less than three months later, in February 2013, another federal

A federal law known as the Gun-Free School Zones Act, passed in 1990 and amended in 1995, prohibits people from carrying firearms on school property. The legislation defined a "school zone" as a distance of 1,000 feet (305 m) from the grounds of a public, parochial or private school, although the law does allow properly licensed individuals to carry firearms on private property adjacent to the school under certain conditions.

court issued a contrary ruling. In a case from Colorado called *Peterson v. Martinez*, the U.S. Tenth Circuit Court of Appeals ruled that the Second Amendment does not give citizens the right to carry a concealed weapon in public.

Most legal observers believe the Supreme Court will eventually decide the issue. However, the Court passed up a chance to do just that in April 2013, when it declined to hear a case challenging New York's strict requirements for obtaining a CCW license, which the NRA likened to "a *de facto* ban on carrying a handgun outside the home."

As of August 2013, New York was one of just nine states with "may issue" concealed-carry laws. In most of these states, it's difficult to obtain a CCW license. Typically the applicant must provide a specific and substantial reason why he or she needs to carry a weapon.

By contrast, in "shall issue" states CCW licenses are granted unless a specific reason (like a criminal record) exists to deny the application. There were 36 shall issue states as of 2014. At that time, an additional five states (Alaska, Arizona, Arkansas, Vermont, and Wyoming) had an unrestricted right to carry, meaning no license is required to tote a concealed weapon. More than a dozen other states were considering legislation for permit-less concealed carry, which some gun rights advocates refer to as "constitutional carry."

States vary widely in the training (if any) they require CCW applicants to undergo. They also place differing restrictions on where a permit-holder may legally take his or her firearm. About 40 states honor CCW permits issued by at least some other states.

One of the gun lobby's major legislative priorities is to replace the hodgepodge of state reciprocity agreements with a federal law requiring any valid concealed-carry permit to be recognized everywhere in the country. The National Right-to-Carry Reciprocity Act has been introduced in Congress in 2009, 2011, and 2012. It was approved overwhelmingly by the House of Representatives in November 2012 and came within three votes of passage in the Senate the following April.

According to the NRA, national CCW reciprocity would "serve as a fundamental protection of the right to self-defense by providing people with the ability to protect themselves not only in their home states, but anywhere they travel where concealed carry is legal."

Opponents, however, say that national reciprocity would impose the permitting standards of the most lax states on everyone else. It would, for example, compel New York City to honor permits issued by Utah—and not just with visitors but also with New York City residents who'd obtained a Utah permit by mail. Local control over who could carry a concealed weapon would effectively be ended. "State and local officials, and police who fight crime on the front lines, should be deciding how to best protect our communities," asserted

Washington, D.C., is one of a handful of jurisdictions in the United States that does not permit private individuals to carry a handgun in public, either concealed or openly. All firearms in the federal district must be registered with the police.

Boston mayor Tom Menino, cochair of Mayors Against Illegal Guns, "not the Washington gun lobby and their allies in Congress."

"THE PRICE OF OUR FREEDOM?"

By any measure, 2012 was a terrible year for mass shootings in the United States. On seven separate occasions, a gunman took the lives of at least four people. There had been three such incidents in 2011, and only one in 2010. In all, according to data compiled by *Mother Jones* magazine, 72 people lost their lives in the 2012 mass shootings. That's a horrifying toll, but it pales in comparison with the approximately 30,000 other Americans killed by guns each year (nearly two-thirds of them suicides).

Mass shootings are comparatively rare. But they invariably spark intense debate about America's gun laws. The gun control and gun rights camps trade claims and counterclaims, restate old arguments, and accuse each other of ignorance or bad faith. After a few days, or perhaps weeks, the country's attention inevitably shifts, and little changes.

The events of December 14, 2012, seemed certain to alter that dynamic. That day, 20-year-old Adam Lanza burst into Sandy Hook Elementary School in Newtown, Connecticut. In about four minutes he fired more than 150 bullets from a semiautomatic rifle, slaughtering 20 first-graders and six adult staff members, before killing himself.

Two days later, President Obama spoke at a prayer vigil in Newtown. "We can't accept events like this as routine," he said. "Are we really prepared to say that we're powerless in the face of such carnage, that the politics are too hard? Are we prepared to say that such violence visited on our children year after year after year is somehow the price of our freedom?" The president pledged to do everything possible to stop similar tragedies from happening again.

The following January, President Obama unveiled a set of gun control proposals that included universal background checks for firearms purchases, a ban on so-called assault weapons, and a limit on the capacity of ammunition magazines. Lanza had used 30-round magazines.

The NRA opposed those measures, as well as every other gun control proposal to emerge in the wake of the Newtown massacre. Its

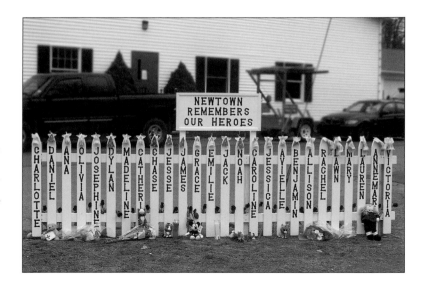

A memorial for the 26 children and adults killed by gunman Adam Lanza at Sandy Hook Elementary School in Newtown, Connecticut, on December 14, 2012. The Sandy Hook shooting was one of the worst incidents of mass murder in U.S. history.

solution to the problem of gun violence was more guns. "The only thing that stops a bad guy with a gun," NRA executive vice president Wayne LaPierre opined, "is a good guy with a gun." The NRA suggested that armed guards be posted at each of the more than 100,000 elementary and secondary schools in the country.

Public opinion overwhelmingly favored new gun control measures, however. A Quinnipiac poll conducted in January and early February 2013 found that 92 percent of Americans supported expanded background checks, 56 percent wanted a ban on assault weapons, and 56 percent backed limiting ammunition clips to 10 rounds.

Eventually a gun control bill emerged in the Senate. The bipartisan Manchin-Toomey bill called for expanded, but not universal, background checks. Gun-show and Internet firearms sales would require a background check, but weapons transferred to family or friends would not. The legislation contained no restrictions on types of weapons or ammunition.

Despite its modest scope, the Manchin-Toomey bill met with vehement opposition from the NRA and almost every other pro-gun group. In the end, the gun rights side prevailed. Though favored by a majority of senators, the bill died in April 2013, when its supporters fell 6 votes short of the 60 required to break a filibuster.

IN THE AFTERMATH OF NEWTOWN

In the absence of federal action, a handful of states passed new gun control laws. New York, for example, made background checks mandatory for all gun transfers except to immediate family members. It required owners of military-style firearms to register their weapons. It instituted background checks for ammunition sales and banned the possession of high-capacity magazines. Connecticut mandated universal background checks, banned 100 assault-style weapons, raised from 18 to 21 the minimum age at which a person can buy a rifle, and limited gun buyers to one firearms purchase per 12 months. Colorado enacted universal background checks and banned sales of high-capacity magazines. Maryland required citizens to take a training course and get a license to buy a gun.

Yet a greater number of states loosened gun laws in the months after the Newtown massacre. By May 2013 at least 16 states had expanded concealed carry. Mississippi opened CCW permits to people as young as 18. Arkansas began allowing permit holders to take their weapons into churches and liquor stores. An Alaska law exempted firearms owned by citizens of the state from federal regulation. In Kansas, the "Second Amendment Protection Act" made any attempt to enforce federal gun laws on firearms manufactured and owned in the Sunflower State a felony punishable by a year in prison. Similar bills were introduced in some three-dozen other state legislatures.

State nullification of federal gun laws, most legal scholars agree, won't pass muster. But the fact that such measures have been considered reflects a growing radicalization in America's gun debate.

A DIFFERENT VISION

Some staunch supporters of the Second Amendment have stepped forward to promote another path. They reject the absolutist approach of the NRA and its allies, insisting instead that the nation can have both strong gun rights and sensible laws to protect public safety.

Former U.S. representative Gabrielle Giffords and her husband, former navy pilot and astronaut Mark Kelly, count themselves among this group. In early 2013 the two lifelong gun owners formed

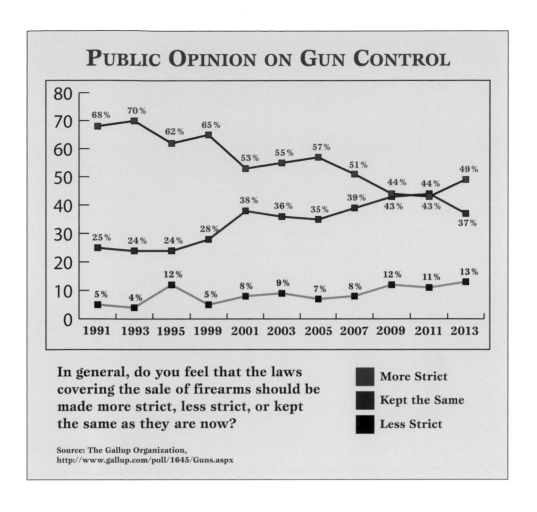

PUBLIC OPINION ON GUN CONTROL

In general, do you feel that the laws covering the sale of firearms should be made more strict, less strict, or kept the same as they are now?

More Strict
Kept the Same
Less Strict

Source: The Gallup Organization,
http://www.gallup.com/poll/1645/Guns.aspx

Americans for Responsible Solutions, which advocates for measures such as universal background checks, restrictions on military-style rifles, and limits on ammunition-magazine capacity. Giffords herself was critically wounded in a 2011 mass shooting in Tucson, Arizona, that claimed six lives.

"I'm a patriot, and I believe the right to bear arms is a definitive part of our American heritage," Giffords wrote in July 2013. "As gun owners, my husband and I understand that the Second Amendment is most at risk when a criminal or deranged person commits a gun crime. These acts only embolden those who oppose gun ownership. Promoting responsible gun laws protects the Second Amendment and reduces lives lost from guns."

Organizations to Contact

Boone and Crockett Club
250 Station Drive
Missoula, MT 59801
Phone: (406) 542-1888
Fax: (406) 542-0784
Email: bcclub@boone-crockett.org
Website: www.boone-crockett.org

Brady Center to Prevent Gun Violence
1225 Eye Street, NW, Suite 1100
Washington, DC 20005
Phone: (202) 289-7319
Fax: (202) 408-1851
Website:
     www.bradycampaign.org

Coalition to Stop Gun Violence
805 15th Street NW, Suite 700
Washington, DC 20005
Phone: (202) 408-0061
Email: csgv@csgv.org
Website: http://csgv.org

Gun Owners of America
8001 Forbes Place, Suite 102
Springfield, VA 22151
Phone: (703) 321-8585
Fax: (703) 321-8408
Website: www.gunowners.org

National Association for Gun Rights
P.O. Box 7002
Fredericksburg, VA 22404
Phone: (877) 405-4570
Fax: (202) 351-0528
Website: www.nationalgun-rights.org

National Association of Certified Firearms Instructors
Tim Grant, President
4722 Forest Circle
Minnetonka, MN 55345
Phone: (952) 935-2414
Email: info@nacfi.us
Website: www.nacfi.us

**National Gun Victims
Action Council**
P.O. Box 10657
Chicago, IL 60610-0657
Email: info@gunvictimsaction.org
Website: http://gunvictimsac-
     tion.org

National Rifle Association
11250 Waples Mill Road
Fairfax, VA 22030
Phone: (800) 672-3888
Fax: (703) 267-3989
Website: www.nra.org

**National Shooting Sports
Foundation**
Flintlock Ridge Office Center
11 Mile Hill Road
Newtown, CT 06470
Phone: (203) 426-1320
Fax: (203) 426-1087
Website: www.nssf.org

**The Second Amendment
Foundation**
12500 NE 10th Place
Bellevue, WA 98005
Phone: (425) 454-7012
Fax: (425) 451-3959
Website: www.saf.org
Email: AdminForWeb@saf.org

Glossary

assault weapon—this term is often used to refer to a semi-automatic firearm that is similar in design and function to military rifles. States that have banned assault weapons each have specific definitions of what firearms are considered to be assault weapons, including those with a combination of several characteristics such as detachable magazines, pistol grips, certain types of stocks, flash suppressors, and other features.

automatic weapon—a firearm that is designed to feed cartridges into the chamber, fire them, eject the empty cases, and repeat this cycle as long as the trigger is depressed and cartridges remain in the magazine or feed system. Examples include true machine guns, submachine guns, selective-fire rifles, and military assault rifles.

background check—an investigation of a gun purchaser's background, usually conducted by state police or the FBI, to determine if the person is prohibited from buying a gun.

ballistics—the science of cartridge discharge and a bullet's flight.

caliber—the diameter of the bore of a gun barrel, usually measured in tenths of an inch or in millimeters.

cartridge—ammunition consisting of a brass case, primer, smokeless powder, and a projectile.

chamber—the part of a firearm at the rear of the barrel where the cartridge is placed before firing.

federal firearms licensee (FFL)—a person who is legally permitted to be in the business of selling firearms in the United States. FFLs are required to conduct background checks before completing any sales, and must comply with federal, state, and local ordinances.

gun show loophole—a term that refers to the undocumented transfer of firearms through private sales, which do not require a background check.

high-capacity magazine—term for any magazine that holds more than 10 cartridges.

long gun—a type of small arm that is designed to be fired while braced against the shoulder, such as a rifle or shotgun.

magazine—a device that holds multiple ammunition cartridges under spring pressure, so they can be rapidly fed into a firearm's chamber.

muzzle—the forward end of the barrel where the projectile exits.

National Instant Criminal Background Check System—a system, managed by the FBI, that searches multiple electronic databases to quickly determine whether a person is eligible to buy firearms.

negligent discharge—the accidental firing of a bullet from a gun. This can usually be avoided by observing the rules of firearm safety.

Saturday night special—a slang phrase that refers in general to any small, inexpensive handgun.

semi-automatic weapon—a type of firearm that has a self-loading action and a magazine that holds multiple ammunition cartridges. When the firearm is loaded and cocked, pulling the trigger fires a cartridge; the firearm action immediately ejects the spent shell, loads a new one into the chamber, and resets the hammer so that the weapon is ready to be fired again the next time the trigger is pulled, until the magazine is empty.

short-barreled firearm—refers to "sawed-off" rifles or shotguns that are illegal under federal law. To be legal in the United States, long guns must have an overal length of 26 inches or more; rifles must have a barrel length of at least 16 inches, while shotgun barrels must be 18 inches or more.

Notes

p. 5   "right most valued . . ." Carl T. Bogus, "The Hidden History of the Second Amendment," *University of California at Davis Law Review* 31 (1998): 312.

p. 7   "You don't feel safe . . ." Claudia Rivero and David Chang, "Local Residents Take a Stand Against Violence," NBC10 Philadelphia, August 8, 2012. http://www.nbcphiladelphia.com/news/local/Local-Residents-Take-a-Stand-Against-Violence-165381966.html

p. 8   "individual whose character . . ." 18 Pa. C.S. § 6109 (e). http://www.legis.state.pa.us/WU01/LI/LI/CT/HTM/18/18.HTM

p. 12   "If somebody has been arrested . . ." Stephanie Farr, "Can't Get a Gun Here? No Problem: Florida Will Issue Permit, and Local Police Must Honor It. Phila. Authorities Are Irate," Philly.com, February 5, 2010. http://articles.philly.com/2010-02-05/news/24955992_1_loophole-gun-firearms

p. 13   "[Someone] could be disapproved . . ." Ibid.

p. 14   "Why would we allow . . ." "EDITORIAL: Closing Fla. Gun Loophole Is a Good Idea," *Delaware County Daily Times*, February 10, 2013. http://www.delcotimes.com/articles/2013/02/10/opinion/doc51187abe064e9121339119.txt?viewmode = fullstory

p. 14   "Why make it harder . . ." Stephanie Farr, "Gun Owners Losing 'Fla. Loophole' Can't Conceal Anger," Philly.com, February 12, 2013. http://articles.philly.com/2013-02-12/news/37041275_1_florida-gun-loophole-parapet-group-gun-owners

p. 14   "You can purchase . . ." Farr, "Can't Get a Gun Here?"

p. 15   "A well regulated Militia . . ." Bill of Rights Transcript Text. http://www.archives.gov/exhibits/charters/bill_of_rights_transcript.html

p. 16   "full and equal benefit . . ." Adam Winkler, "The Secret History of Guns," *The Atlantic* (Sept. 2011): 84.

p. 18   "reasonable, sensible . . ." Ibid., 86.

p. 18   "We do not think . . ." Jon Michaud, "The Birth of the Modern Gun Debate," *The New Yorker* (April 19, 2012). http://www.newyorker.com/online/blogs/backissues/2012/04/the-birth-of-the-modern-gun-debate.html

p. 20   "only firewall standing . . ." National Rifle Association website.
         http://home.nra.org/membership

p. 20   "the measure as a whole . . ." Winkler, "Secret History of Guns," 87.

p. 21   "the firm conclusion . . ." Winkler, "Secret History of Guns," 83.

p. 23   "time, attention, and labor . . ." James B. Jacobs, *Can Gun Control Work?*
         (New York: Oxford University Press, 2002), 24.

p. 33   "How hard is it . . ." John Lott, " 'False Positives' from Brady Law Bar Gun
         Ownership," *Newsmax*, June 14, 2011.
         http://www.newsmax.com/JohnLott/bradylaw-gunowner-
         ship/2011/06/14/id/399967

p. 36   "The answer is . . ." "Mayor Michael Bloomberg Says 40 Percent of Guns
         Are Sold Without a Background Check," PolitiFact.com, July 25, 2012
         (updated January 30, 2013). http://www.politifact.com/truth-o-
         meter/statements/2012/jul/25/michael-bloomberg/mayor-michael-
         bloomberg-says-40-percent-guns-are-s/

p. 36   "It is hard to believe . . ." John Lott, "The '40 Percent' Myth," *National
         Review Online*, January 24, 2013. http://www.nationalreview.com/arti-
         cles/338735/40-percent-myth-john-lott

p. 38   "Bonnie had inquired . . ." Gun Owners of America, "GOA Laments First
         'Brady Victim,'" Gun Owners of America website, March 30, 2001.
         http://gunowners.org/pr0104.htm

p. 39   "I believe [Fendry] . . . Mike Nichols, "Victim's Brother Criticizes
         Lobbyist," *Milwaukee Journal*, May 14, 1991, p. B1.
         http://news.google.com/newspapers?nid = 1499&dat = 19910514&id = 2es
         bAAAAIBAJ&sjid = NiwEAAAAIBAJ&pg = 6366,5012412

p. 39   "the evidence is insufficient . . ." Robert A. Hahn et al., "Firearms Laws
         and the Reduction of Violence: A Systematic Review," *American Journal of
         Preventive Medicine* vol. 28, 2S1(2005): 52.

p. 40   "none of the funds . . ." Michael Luo, "N.R.A. Stymies Firearms Research,
         Scientists Say," *New York Times*, January 25, 2011.
         http://www.nytimes.com/2011/01/26/us/26guns.html?pagewanted = 1&_r
         = 0

p. 40   "You'd think that after . . ." Alex Seitz-Wald, "The NRA's War on Gun
         Science," *Salon*, July 25, 2012.
         http://www.salon.com/2012/07/25/the_nras_war_on_gun_science/

p. 42   "New York gun laws . . ." Michael Wilson, "Legal Guns en Route to New
         York Are Cause for Arrest Before Flight Home," *New York Times*, June 9,
         2013. http://www.nytimes.com/2013/06/10/nyregion/lawful-handguns-

departing-for-new-york-but-unlawful-upon-arrival.html?pagewanted = all

p. 42   "No one should ever . . ." Stephanie Mencimer, "Go Ahead, Make Mark Meckler's Day," *Mother Jones*, January 13, 2012. http://www.mother-jones.com/politics/2012/01/mark-meckler-tea-party-gun-reciprocity

p. 45   "The Supreme Court has decided . . ." Ray Long, Annie Sweeney and Monique Garcia, "Concealed Carry: Court Strikes Down Illinois' Ban," *Chicago Tribune*, December 11, 2012. http://articles.chicagotribune.com/2012-12-11/news/chi-us-appeals-court-strikes-down-states-concealedcarry-ban-20121211_1_court-strikes-appeals-court-david-sigale

p. 46   "a *de facto* ban . . ." Adam Liptak, "Justices Refuse Case on Gun Law in New York," *New York Times*, April 15, 2013. http://www.nytimes.com/2013/04/16/us/politics/supreme-court-declines-gun-law-case.html?_r = 0

p. 47   "serve as a fundamental . . ." NRA Institute for Legislative Action, "'National Right to Carry Reciprocity Act of 2012' Introduced in U.S. Senate," NRA-ILA website, March 13, 2012. http://www.nraila.org/legisla-tion/federal-legislation/2012/national-right-to-carry-reciprocity-act-of-2012-introduced-in-us-senate.aspx

p. 47   "State and local officials . . ." Sally Kalson, "Guns, Guns for Everyone," *Pittsburgh Post-Gazette*, September 25, 2011. http://www.post-gazette.com/stories/life/sally-kalson/guns-guns-for-everyone-316339/

p. 48   "We can't accept . . ." Transcript: President Obama at Sandy Hook Prayer Vigil, December 16, 2012. http://www.npr.org/2012/12/16/167412995/transcript-president-obama-at-sandy-hook-prayer-vigil

p. 49   "The only thing that stops . . ." Peter Overby, "NRA: 'Only Thing That Stops a Bad Guy with a Gun Is a Good Guy with a Gun,'" National Public Radio, *All Things Considered*, December 21, 2012. http://www.npr.org/2012/12/21/167824766/nra-only-thing-that-stops-a-bad-guy-with-a-gun-is-a-good-guy-with-a-gun

p. 51   "I'm a patriot . . ." Gabrielle Giffords, "Gabrielle Giffords: Gun Rights Come with Responsibilities," *USA Today*, July 1, 2013. http://www.usato-day.com/story/opinion/2013/07/01/gabrielle-giffords-gun-rights-col-umn/2480751/

Further Reading

Bussard, Michael E. *NRA Firearms Sourcebook: Your Ultimate Guide to Guns, Ballistics, and Shooting.* Fairfax, Va.: National Rifle Association, 2006.

Carter, Gregg Lee, ed. *Guns in American Society: An Encyclopedia of History, Politics, Culture, and the Law.* 2nd ed. Santa Barbara, Calif.: ABC-CLIO, 2012.

Gregersen, Steven D. *The Gun Guide for Those Who Know Nothing About Firearms.* New York: CreateSpace, 2012.

Halbrook, Stephen P. *The Founders' Second Amendment: Origins of the Right to Bear Arms.* Oakland, Calif.: Independent Institute, 2012.

Jacobs, James B. *Can Gun Control Work?* New York: Oxford University Press, 2002.

Leghorn, Nick. *Getting Started with Firearms in the United States: A Complete Guide for Newbies.* New York: CreateSpace, 2012.

Lott, John R. *More Guns, Less Crime: Understanding Crime and Gun Control Laws.* Chicago: University of Chicago Press, 2010.

Spitzer, Robert J. *The Politics of Gun Control.* 5th ed. Washington, D.C.: CQ Press, 2011.

Whitney, Craig R. *Living with Guns: A Liberal's Case for the Second Amendment.* New York: Public Affairs, 2012.

Winkler, Adam. *Gunfight: The Battle Over the Right to Bear Arms in America.* New York: W. W. Norton & Co., 2011.

Internet Resources

http://www.fbi.gov/about-us/cjis/nics/reports/2012-operations-report

A detailed report from the FBI on the operations of the National Instant Criminal Background Check System (NICS).

http://www.bradycampaign.org

The Brady Campaign to Prevent Gun Violence advocates for gun control laws.

http://www.nraila.org

The website of the Institute for Legislative Action, the lobbying arm of the National Rifle Association. This site includes a state-by-state overview of laws related to firearms ownership.

http://smartgunlaws.org

The California-based Law Center to Prevent Gun Violence provides information on federal and state firearms laws, analysis of relevant court decisions, and pro-gun-control policy recommendations.

http://www.handgunlaw.us

This site is regularly updated with information about state and federal statutes related to firearms ownership.

www.atf.gov

Information on federal and state regulations with regard to firearms ownership is available on the Bureau of Alcohol, Tobacco, Firearms and Explosives (ATF) website.

http://www.nrainstructors.org/searchcourse.aspx

This searchable database enables you to find a certified NRA shooting and safety instructor in your local area.

http://www.boone-crockett.org

Boone and Crockett Club is an organization that promotes wildlife conservation and hunter safety. It was founded by Theodore Roosevelt in 1887, making it the oldest such organization in the United States.

http://www.nssf.org/safety

The National Shooting Sports Foundation's web page on firearms safety includes educational videos and articles about safe and responsible gun ownership.

Index

Numbers in **bold italic** refer to captions.

About the Author

John Ziff is a freelance writer and editor. His books include *Causes of World War I* (OTTN Publishing, 2005) and *Espionage and Treason* (Chelsea House, 2000). He lives near Philadelphia.